S0-EKA-411

all color book of Cats

CRESCENT BOOKS
NEW YORK

Contents

The Nature of Cats

Cats are as individual as people and they are perhaps the most independent of all animals. Unlike dogs, a cat can never be made to do anything to which it objects. It is often said that some dogs and their owners are so devoted to each other that they look alike. This does not apply to cat owners, and although cats can be just as devoted as dogs to their homes and own people, they never seem to take on an owner's personality – they have enough of their own.

Many cats can perform clever tricks and can open doors, windows and cupboards with dexterity. Siamese and Burmese are particularly agile; they will beg, retrieve, and perform wonderful dances and jumps when they find suitable playthings. Sometimes they will knock the telephone receiver off when it rings in an attempt, we suppose, to answer it.

Cats like to be flattered and to be told they are beautiful and clever; it is quite certain that they understand what is said, and they react very definitely to anger and cruelty. Cats dislike high voices and violent noises; they like flowers and are attracted by bright colours. After many years of observing cats I cannot believe, as some do, that cats see only in black and white. Black and Tabby cats definitely like bright red and yellow, white cats and Siamese are attracted to blue and mauve and I am sure that they choose the colours that complement them.

Cats communicate more than most animals with humans and with each other by the way they move their ears and tails. They have many eloquent facial expressions and can portray disapproval, fear, anger, pleasure and many other emotions. A cat's voice is most expressive, and can indicate all the various moods. They can be demanding, cajoling, bullying or merely conversational, they leave you in no doubt when they are hungry or cross or disapproving, and equally there is no mistaking their purr of happiness, a sound made only by cats, large and small. Siamese in particular will growl like a dog on occasion and they can be excellent watch dogs, growling when anyone approaches their home. A Siamese in season has to be heard to be believed and the Burmese is almost as noisy, but most other breeds are quieter. Some are almost silent and have to be watched closely if you do not want them to get out and find their own mate. When males fight the noise is frightful, reminiscent of the jungle.

Except for some white cats which are born deaf, a cat's hearing is acute, and their ears will pick up the slightest sound. Ears also indicate a cat's mood; a flick acknowledges that you have been heard, but when the ears are flattened and lie close to the head it is a danger signal and it is wiser not to handle a cat when in such a mood. When they are angry they fluff their tails out to twice the normal size, and a ridge of fur standing up along the spine shows that the cat is more than ready to fight.

Never laugh at a cat because they hate it, although they are always more than willing to make fun of their owners and Siamese in particular have a great sense of humour. The Burmese, too, have a sense of fun and will play with pieces of string and paper even when quite old. Never give cats or kittens plastic toys, because if swallowed, they can cause obstruction in the intestines which may be fatal. The toy most cats enjoy is a large rabbit or hare's foot, which may be obtained from a poulterer's, and should be well scrubbed before being given to your pet.

Cats walk on their toes, and are notorious for their ability to walk completely silently. They can do this because they retract, or draw in their claws, all except the Siamese, that is – their claws are like those of the dog – unretractable. Consequently they do not walk silently, are more clumsy than other cats and are not adept at landing softly in a small space. Several Siamese cats and kittens rushing about can give the impression that they are wearing hob-nailed boots!

It is said that cats can see in the dark, and though this fact has been disputed, it is certain that cats, wild and domestic, do hunt at night and travel many miles when it is dark, so it is only cats

who know what they really can do. Eyes are a sure indication of health; they should be bright and alert, and the nose should be cool and moist to the touch. Cats are clean and fastidious, so you should help to keep their coats free from fleas and their ears clean, or they will be very miserable and unhealthy. Cats can be very brave and there are many stories of instances when they have awakened people to warn them of fire, or leaking gas, or floods. They are particularly courageous when they have kittens, and if danger threatens they will never leave their kittens and go to the greatest lengths to get them to a safe place.

One of the most famous cats was one who lived through the London air raids of the last war, a small Tabby and White called Faith. She had walked into St Augustine's Church, in Watling Street as a stray kitten, and as she

was never claimed and would not leave, the Rector took her to live in the Rectory House adjoining the Church. In September 1940, Faith had a black and white kitten called Panda, and the two of them were comfortably installed on the top floor of the Rectory House. Later that month, however, the cat became restless and agitated and went on a tour of inspection of the rest of the house, eventually taking the kitten out of the basket and installing it in a room three floors below at the other side of the house. When the Rector found the empty basket he searched for the cats and took them upstairs. Faith at once seized the kitten and took it downstairs again. The Rector took the kitten upstairs four times and then gave up the struggle. Three nights later the blitz began and a bomb went through the roof of the Rectory House, which blazed

and crumbled. The Rector returned to find his house a mass of burning ruins, but in spite of firemen saying it was hopeless he started to search for the cat. He called Faith several times, never expecting an answer, but to his relief he heard a faint cry from the smouldering ruins in answer. Peering down he saw the brave little cat sitting there entirely hemmed in by rubble. She was serene and unafraid, and had the kitten between her paws. He hacked a passage out of the debris and then coaxed the cat and her kitten out. Both were begrimed but unhurt. Faith was taken to the Church vestry just before the whole Church house collapsed in ruins. There she stayed and calmly settled down with her kitten, knowing they were safe, which indeed they were, as the Church was not hit. She was the first cat to win decorations for courage.

Previous page: left In the Middle Ages the cat was linked with the Devil. Hundreds of people were tortured on suspicion of being witches and the cats, who were supposed to be their familiars, were tortured and burned as well. In Britain, the black cat is supposed to be lucky, especially if it runs across your path, though some people think the good fortune is only released if you stroke the cat three times.

Right The cat is built for great speed. Although it is most often seen lazily relaxing this is because it really is a nocturnal animal. When the cat is hunting it moves quickly and silently, covering the ground in great leaps. The way the cat runs is similar to a giraffe or camel. First the front and back legs on one side move, then the front and back legs on the other. This is what gives the smooth gliding movement, unlike other animals which appear to jog along. The Foreign White Cat in the picture demonstrates clearly how the line of the back stays parallel to the ground.

***

Top left 'Curiosity killed the cat.' So goes the old saying which must be far from true because the cat is a naturally cautious animal. Without doubt it is an inquisitive creature but it would not take unnecessary risks to satisfy that curiosity. This cat peering over a bank will not emerge completely until he has surveyed the landscape. There may be something nasty about.

Bottom left 'All clear? Then I am coming over.' Whilst the cat will not rush headlong into situations without first taking stock, it is not a timid creature. Unlike the dog, which will usually rush off in the face of danger, the cat will stand its ground. By arching its back to make itself look bigger than it really is, snarling, hissing and spitting, it looks a formidable opponent. Most dogs will not stay to face such a bundle of fury.

Right Kittens and cats are very expressive creatures, and they can portray their many different moods with their voices, eyes, ears and even with their tails. A flick of an ear, a twitch of a tail and you know that your words have been acknowledged. That this tabby kitten wants something is evident in the line of his head, the arch of his back, the curve of his tail and the delicate pointing of his paws. He is politely saying that what he wants is very urgent.

Left Long ago in Arabia, so it is written, the Prophet Mohammed had for his pet a little white cat he called 'Muezza.' While Mohammed preached from the tallest minaret in Mecca the cat would curl up to sleep in the sleeve of his robes. Once, when he was called to prayer, Mohammed cut off his sleeve rather than disturb the sleeping animal.

Below When you provide your dog with a basket that is his place for a nap at all times. A cat, on the other hand, can curl up and sleep anywhere and in the most awkward positions. This white cat is dozing and sunbathing though it does look as if he might wake up with a terrible headache.

9

Right A really good stretch is enjoyed by all cats, and it literally is a stretch for they appear to increase their length by a third again. A cat has tremendous muscular energy and flexibility. There are more than five hundred muscles in its body to give the cat its splendid elasticity.

Below Cats love to be near grass. They love the gentle movement as the grass is caught in the breeze, they enjoy hunting the insects that abound in the undergrowth, and they like to eat grass too, as this is a natural medicine. For town cats with no access to a grassy patch it is important to provide grass grown in pots or boxes. Crow's-foot grass seems to be a great favourite and a fresh supply should be sown every week or ten days.

Left 'Cool Cats and Tom Cats, we are gathered together here this evening to make a protest on behalf of cats in cartoons who are badly treated by mice. This nonsense gives a false view of the intelligence of our kind and I should like to table a motion to this effect.'

Right 'Thank you, one and all, but please will you save your applause until the end of the meeting. If we are able to make our voice heard we must all howl together. There is tremendous loss of face for our species whenever one member is outwitted by a mere mouse, which is in any case an impossibility.'

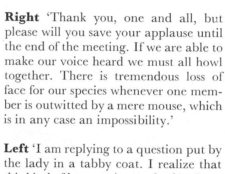

Left 'I am replying to a question put by the lady in a tabby coat. I realize that this kind of humour is popular but I am sure you will agree with me when I say that we cats do not like being laughed at. Like all of my friends here I enjoy a good joke but all this has really gone too far.'

Right 'How dare you, Sir, imply that I have called this meeting because I am jealous. I have no aspirations to fame, nor do I resent not having been asked to take a star part in any film. We cats must stand together or before we know it someone will write a story about a cat being frightened by a spider.'

Right 'If you would like to become a member of my organization for the Preservation of the Dignity of Cats, my secretary will be pleased to send you details. Thank you all for your kind attention.'

Opposite White cats have a tendency to deafness, particularly when the cat has blue eyes. It is thought that black cats with orange eyes may have been introduced into the mating pattern to transfer the orange eyes to the white cats. It is difficult to achieve a really vivid orange but it is very striking when it does occur.

Above 'I may only be a small cat but my claws are strong and if you come any closer I shall be forced to use them.' The cat's claws are curved and very sharp. They are well adapted for the cat to grasp its prey or for it to get a firm grip on a smooth surface when it is climbing. The claws can be extended or retracted by means of flexor tendons. When the claws are not in use they are hidden in openings at the end of the digits so that they are protected from wear and tear, thus remaining sharp for when they are needed.

Left Cats are naturally fastidious creatures. They cannot bear to feel anything messy or sticky in their coat and they will spend a great deal of time washing and cleaning themselves. The tongue of the cat is covered with rasp-like protuberances which give the tongue that rough feeling and enables the cat to lick its coat clean. With its great flexibility the cat can reach most parts of its body with its tongue, except, of course, its head and this it washes by licking its paw and wiping the head and face over with this. It is wise, however, to groom all domestic cats every day, as it is very good for them and many also enjoy it.

Right Cats love to lie in the sun. They usually have a favourite spot because they have the knack for finding a place where it is sheltered and warm, and this they make their own. It is thought that this love of warmth first brought cat and Man together when Man's camp fire attracted the cat to the comfort of its flames.

Pedigrees

The English cats today consist of the Persians or Long-hairs, the British and Foreign Short-hairs and the Siamese, which are always in a category of their own. In the early days of the Cat Fancy the British Short-hair was the most numerous and popular; there were a few Angoras and a few Blue, Black, Red and Tabby Persians; Siamese were very rare and many of the breeds that are popular today had not been heard of.

The principal breeds are Longhaired; Black, White with blue or orange eyes, Blue, Red Self, Cream, Smoke, Tortoiseshell and Tortoiseshell and White, Blue Cream, Brown, Red and Silver Tabby, Chinchilla, Colourpoint and Bi-coloured. Shaded Silvers are not recognized in England, which is a pity. The latest additions are the Turkish cat, which is white with auburn markings, and the French blue-eyed Birman with Seal, Blue, Chocolate or Lilac Points. These two breeds have longer heads and noses and larger ears than the Persians and their coats are not so long, though their tails are as bushy. It is interesting to note that in Sweden Turkish cats are also found with Tortoiseshell, Red, and Tortoiseshell and White colouring; type

is the same. These breeds are not yet as popular as the older ones, but numbers are gradually increasing. The Birmans, which are the same as Colourpoints with additional white socks create great interest, they also have sweet, amiable natures.

Today the pedigree British Short-hair has declined in popularity, but interest in them never really dies out and in every show you can see worthy representatives of most of the colour varieties. Perhaps the most popular are Blacks, Whites, Silver Tabbies and Silver Spotteds. British Blues and Tortoiseshell and Whites, Creams, Blue Creams, Tortoiseshells, Brown and Red Tabbies and Bi-coloureds are rather scarce, although I am happy to say that we are now seeing some excellent Brown Spotteds and Brown and Red Tabbies. Manx cats have phases of popularity; few have been seen for the past two years, but they will be back again. These clever and curious little cats, like some of the British Short-hairs are not money-makers and are kept only by people who really love the breed, which is as it should be.

The Foreign Short-hairs are always around, although our oldest breeds, the Russian Blues and

Abyssinians, are not very numerous. The most popular at the moment are the Brown Burmese, followed by the Blue Burmese. These were the only two colours until breeders imported two Champagne coloured cats from America and a Chocolate coloured one from Canada. Now other colours are appearing: Cream, Blue Cream, Champagne, Chocolate, and Lilac (known in America as Frost). These new colour varieties are not yet recognized by the British Governing Council, but have subsidiary breed numbers. Burmese are a fascinating breed and are the only serious rivals to the Siamese.

The Havanas are gaining in popularity, and are an interesting breed of Siamese type with bright green eyes and a wistful expression. The best examples have coats the colour of a polished chestnut, and are not nearly so dark as the Brown Burmese. The most recent recognitions are the Cornish and Devon Rex; they have fought their way up since the 'fifties and there are now the two separate varieties, with their own breed numbers and standard of points. Like the Manx, their coats can be of any colour; many have really lovely curly coats, the whites are like woolly lambs and the neuters in particular are very handsome. With only a very few exceptions, they all have sweet dispositions. There are a few Si-Rex, bred from a Siamese and a Rex; the good specimens are of Rex type, with blue eyes and the Seal Point colouring.

The Foreign Whites have pure white coats and lovely blue eyes; of Siamese type, they have been mysteriously bred from British Whites, Siamese and Havanas. They are very beautiful, easy to handle and are awaiting recognition by the Council. The Chartreux is a well-built cat of similar type to the British Blue. It is seen on the Continent and has a rather

soft, dark blue coat and yellow eyes. The Lion-clawed or poly-dactyl cat, usually a Tabby, has six toes and is also a very handsome and well-built cat.

The various American cat magazines are fascinating to read. Notices of studs, queens and kittens abound; much space is given to advertizing the many and varied items designed especially for cats: blankets, feeding utensils, movable pens, jewelled collars and harness, heated beds, litter and litter trays, many brands of pet foods, disinfectants and medicants of all kinds. There is even a pussy playhouse with wall-to-wall catnip carpeting. Unluckily, the British Fancy has only one official paper which records principal shows, judges' reports, etc. but cannot deal with the kind of detail given in the American publications.

The Cat Fancy in the USA recognizes the same breeds of cats as we do, though not always by the same name, as well as several more. The Colourpoint is known as the Himalayan, and there are many more colour varieties of the breed. The Russian Blue is known as the Maltese and the Tortoise-shell and White, both the Long-haired and the Short-haired versions is known as the Calico cat. Angoras are to be found on the American show benches, but not here. These cats are said to have originated from Angora in Western Asia, and were great favourites with the Turks. They had long, silky, white, fine hair coats and blue eyes, and were very docile. Although we do not see them in England now, they were often brought here by ship 150 years ago. They were sold in Leadenhall Market in East London and were priced at £5. Many of our Long-haired Blues, Whites, Creams and Chinchillas are exported to the USA, together with Colourpoints and the French Birmans of the same type as the Turkish, with good blue eyes and white gloved feet.

The American Fancy recognizes the Peke-Faced Tabby, the Tortie Long-hair, the Shaded Silvers and the Maine Coon cats, which are a popular and distinctive breed. There is also a Long-haired Blue Tabby and the Kymer, which I have seen on the Continent, and which can really be described as a Long-haired Siamese, as type and colouring are similar. A great many other colours are recognized, such as the variously coloured Cameos, the Red Smokes, Self-Chocolates, Self-Lilacs, and the Tibetan Temple Cat, which rather resembles the Kymer.

Short-hairs follow the same coat pattern as the English cats: Black, White, Blue, Manx, Rex and Siamese. Another Blue is the Korat cat, said to have come from Thailand; it has a fairly heavy body, a heart-shaped mask and very brilliant yellow-green eyes. They are rather scarce as efforts are made to keep the breed pure. Other breeds of cats advertized in American journals are Japanese Bobtails, Balinese, Egyptian Mau, Tonkinese with blue eyes, described as milk and honey cats, all fascinating cats, carefully maintained by the breeders.

Previous page: left The Long-haired Cream is a very attractive breed of cat. It is most important that the colour should be a rich, slightly warm-toned ivory, without it becoming too red. When this happens the experts describe it as hot, and it is considered a fault to have a hot cream colour. The aim of the breeder is to produce a pale, clear colour, and each hair must be coloured the same from the tip to the root.

Right The Cameo Cat is recognized in the United States of America as a breed but not so in Britain. There are four Cameos, Shell, Shaded, Smoke and Tabby. They conform to the standards for Persians and the pattern is the same as that of Chinchilla and Silvers. The tipping on the long, pale coat is red to give a tinsel appearance.

Top left The first Abyssinian Cat was brought to Britain by the wife of a British Army Officer. There are no cats in Abyssinia today that answer to the description so the origins are really unknown. There is nothing cobby or British about this cat for it is lithe and long and because there is something very lion-like in its appearance, it is sometimes called the 'Little Lion Cat'.

Bottom left This lovely little Odd-eyed White cannot be shown in a class of its own in Britain because it is not a recognized breed. In America, however, the Odd-eyed White has a breed class and number. These unusual cats are the result of a cross-mating between Blue-eyed Whites and Orange-eyed Whites, when the breeders have been endeavouring to breed out the tendency to deafness in white cats with blue eyes. Some owners of white cats with one blue eye and one orange eye believe that the cat can only hear on the side with the orange eye but there is no evidence to support this.

Right At one time New Englanders thought that the Maine Coon Cat was a cross between a cat and a racoon but such an idea is quite inconceivable. The coat of a Coon Cat resembles that of a raccoon and the legs show a slight toeing-in rather like that animal, and it is from this that the cat gets its name. The head is pointed and the eyes often show a slight slant, even though the shape of the eyes is perfectly round. The Long-haired Tabbies that went to America with the early settlers are thought to be the ancestors of the Maine Coon Cat.

Left A cat which actually comes from Thailand is the Korat Cat. It is a Siamese type of cat which is solid grey in colour with amber-green eyes. Although rare in Thailand, a male and female were taken from there to the United States and now Korats are beginning to make an appearance at the shows. Several generations of breeding true, however, must pass before they become an accepted breed.

Below The Himalayan Cat of the United States and the British Colour-point are basically the same. It is a Persian cat to which the Siamese colouring has been transferred. Breeders in several countries experimented over a long period to obtain a long-haired Siamese. One of the most attractive features of the Siamese is its slim elegance, but this 'foreign' type did not look right with long hair. It took a long time to achieve the delicate Siamese colouring and at the same time eliminate the type.

Right The Black Long-haired Cat is one of the oldest of the pedigree breeds. Unfortunately it has a coat which can easily become shabby, and it is very difficult to keep it in first class condition. The standard calls for the coat to be raven or jet black. Black cats who frequently get their feet wet as a result of walking through grass tend to get rusty marks about their paws and legs, and strong sunshine can have a bleaching effect on the coat.

Below It was in 1950 that the first Rex kitten appeared. A pair of cats on a farm in Cornwall produced a very peculiar kitten with a curly coat. All other cats have straight hair, whether it is long or short. Because it was so unusual the owner mated it back with its mother. More curly kittens were the result and thus began the Cornish Rex breed. Less than ten years after the appearance of the Cornish Rex a curly coated kitten made its appearance in Devon. There was no connection between the two and successive experiments showed that they were the result of different genetic mutations. Now the Cornish Rex and Devon Rex are separate established breeds.

Right The Chinchilla is one of the loveliest of all cats. The first impression is that it is white but closer inspection shows that each individual hair is tipped with black. This gives the Chinchilla its characteristic sparkling silver appearance. Since the cat is ethereal, never coarse, there is something almost fairy-like about the Chinchilla. In America the breed is split into three classes so that there is also the Shaded Silver and the Masked Silver. These two cats are more heavily ticked than the Chinchilla so that where the one looks like silver the others look more like pewter.

Below In the United States of America some people like to keep exotic cats for pets. This is a jungle cat which has been domesticated. They come mostly from pet shops as they are nearly always jungle born, few are bred by cat fanciers. The most common are the Ocelot and Margay, which make very impressive and unusual pets.

Below The Manx Cat has no tail. Some people say that long ago the tails were used to decorate the shields of Irish warriors and rather than have this happen the anxious mother cat bit them off her kittens at birth. It is also said that Noah cut the tail off the cat as he slammed the door of the Ark – the cat was the last animal to enter. These stories are, of course, legend. Tailless cats are to be found in many parts of the world and the supposition that they originated on the Isle of Man is also without foundation.

Right The Siamese is affectionate and loves to be in the company of humans. It is extremely intelligent and is usually very demanding. This is not the cat to choose if you have to be out of the house for long periods. In fact, the Siamese would much prefer to accompany you on your outings and it can easily be trained to walk on a lead. This of course, should be started whilst your pet is still a kitten as grown cats will not accept a collar without a struggle, but there is a distinct advantage when you go on long journeys as the cat can be exercised without fear of losing it.

Left It is strange how so many of the alley cats seem to be black and white, though this must not make us have less respect for a true Bi-coloured Cat. These cats are difficult to breed with the colour in the correct proportions and in the right places. The difficulty in achieving the correct pattern made these cats almost disappear from the shows. Fortunately they are making a comeback, and have just received recognition in Britain for a second time. Colours for the standard may be black, cream, blue or orange, all with white as the second colour.

Below The most important feature in Tabby Cats is the distinctness and correct placing of the marking, it is also important to see that the colours are quite separate, the black must not become mixed with the ground colour. The ground colour of this Tabby is pure silver. The kitten shows how the tail should be neatly ringed.

Right New Englanders call the Tortoise-shell and White, both long-haired and short-haired, Calico Cats. Males are extremely rare and the breed cannot be produced to order, as the genetic pattern is unpredictable.

Living with a Cat

If you are thinking of buying a pedigree kitten for a pet, or perhaps with a view to breeding and showing, make your choice carefully. If you live in a flat or house in a built-up area, it is often best to choose a placid British Short-haired cat as they are contented, easy to manage and, if neutered, will grow into handsome cats. You will need more time to look after a Long-hair as their coats require very careful grooming. If you have a comparatively rare breed your responsibilities are much greater unless you have it neutered or speyed. Some breeds need more exercise than others; one of these is the Abyssinian cat, which is very active and should be allowed plenty of freedom. They are happiest in the country, although they face a very real hazard of being shot in mistake for rabbits. All the Orientals are great individualists, demanding attention and companionship as well as freedom. The Russian Blue has a quieter temperament and would be happy to spend most of its time indoors with its owner. Rex cats make excellent pets, being very tough and healthy, and give their owners a dog-like devotion. They are easy to manage and will eat anything. The Cornish type usually have

thicker coats, but the Devon have the cute pixie expression which appeals to many people. Both the Cornish and the Devon Rex also make beautiful neuters. However, they can be jealous, a characteristic they share with Siamese cats, and if they are kept with other animals they must never be overlooked. They also have small voices.

All cats, however, need space and should not be overcrowded or they will not thrive; unlike dogs, they do not have the herd instinct and, unless brought up together, may really dislike one another. If you have adult cats and wish to introduce another, it is much wiser to get a kitten as after a short time the adult cats will accept it, but it is a difficult and tiring job to fit in an adult cat. In fact, it may never settle in at all. If cats have to spend their time indoors arrange to have a wire netting window-frame or frames made, so that the windows can be opened in good weather, especially in a sunny room. If your pets can have the use of a garden, wire a part of it in if possible. Cats and kittens are inquisitive, and will stray quite long distances. Though they will always return they may be killed on the roads on the way back and

in many areas the number of stolen cats is increasing, so safeguard your pet. Burmese in particular, probably the most playful and curious of all cats, have a tendency to wander away and have been known to be absent for days; unluckily, they do not always return.

You may not wish to own a pedigree kitten; you may be given a non-pedigree kitten or you may fall for one in a pet shop, but whatever you have they all need the same care and attention. Brush and comb your pets daily; it is not only necessary to keep the coat free from fleas, but cats really enjoy their grooming, as they are fundamentally very clean and cannot always cope with their coats themselves, particularly if they are long-haired. They can become anaemic and miserable if kept in dirty or overcrowded conditions.

Always provide more than one sanitary tray for kittens as they will need to use them frequently. They must be cleaned often as cats and kittens will not use dirty trays and will find other places. Newspaper can be used, or cat litter which can be bought at pet shops. It is better to have a special bin for used litter; put it in a plastic bag and seal it up, and it can then be put in the dustbin. If peat is used this can be put on the compost heap, but do not burn the used litter as the smell is very unpleasant and you will be unpopular with neighbours.

If you are out all day, try to have two kittens, as they will be company for one another and will thrive better if not bored and lonely. It is wiser not to take kittens until they are at least ten weeks old unless you can be around all the time to see that they get four small meals daily. It is not a good plan to leave a plateful of food in the morning to last until evening, as the kittens will invariably eat it all up at once, will be very hungry by evening and then will bolt their evening meal. This will give them indigestion and probably sickness and they can become quite ill very quickly.

They need a milk and Farex meal with a little fish morning and afternoon, and two protein meals midday and evening. Do not give a lot of milk – about a tablespoon of undiluted tinned milk at each meal is all that is needed. They should have a little minced cooked meat – beef is best – for the mid-day meal, and raw meat at night. Obviously as the kittens grow they can have larger meals, and will not need the afternoon milk dish and can start having vege-tables and fish mixed into their diet. Carrots are particularly good mashed up and added to the cooked meat meal. They will eventually reject the morning milk meal as well and want to have meat or fish instead. How-ever do not give too much raw meat, as it will be too rich for them. A little olive or corn oil daily is liked by some cats, and is especially good for Rex. You can also give grated cheddar cheese and as they grow up they will love dry cat biscuits – there are several varieties on the market. It is very important to always leave fresh water down in a heavy bowl so that it cannot easily be knocked over.

A scratching post is a necessity and will save your furniture. Do not give cats soft rubber toys, nor anything made of plastic, nor chicken, rabbit or chop bones, as they can be very dangerous if swallowed.

If you intend to take up breed-ing start in a small way with not more than two kittens, and then only if you are able to give your pets a great deal of attention, otherwise it is really better to have them neutered. I would ad-vise that you keep females to begin with and do not attempt to keep

a male as a stud until you have experience of breeding. The most important thing is to find a good stud that will suit and complement your cat's breeding; any old cat will not do if you want to breed kittens that will do well on the show bench and be strong and healthy as well. You can get advice about this and do not think that because a cat is a champion you must use him; champions are often overworked. Never leave your queen where the stud's quarters are grubby and where there is no adequate pen for the queen to live in until she is ready to mate, it is really best to visit the stud's home yourself and see the conditions he is living in. Do not let your queen have more than two litters in a year, especially if Burmese or Siamese, as they tend to have big litters of five, six and seven kittens, and females can become exhausted if allowed to breed every time they come into season. Incidentally both these breeds can be very

noisy, particularly when they call, and are not suitable for flats, as the noise they make will probably annoy other people in the house.

Cat breeding can be an interesting and absorbing hobby, provided one is not tempted to keep too many cats, and also is not dependent on selling the kittens as it is often difficult to place them in suitable homes. They should be inoculated from the age of ten weeks, and not sold until this has been done.

If you are going to show your cats you will have to groom them for show presentation. White cats must be kept very clean from the beginning, as dingy coats and yellowed tails are not acceptable, and it is not possible to eradicate these faults in one season of grooming. If kept in good trim, powdering should be all that is necessary, but a bath overnight is sometimes needed. Care must be taken over this and it must be done in time for the cat to become thoroughly dry, to avoid

a chill, before being taken out of its home. Powder cannot be used for dark coated cats, but a bran bath is useful for all colours. The bran must be completely brushed and combed out and on the light coloured cats the coat can be finished off with powder. Dark coated cats can be wiped over with eau-de-cologne, and a final polish can be given to short-haired cats with a wash leather or a piece of silk. When you take your cat to a show, be sure that its coat is free from fleas and that the ears are perfectly clean, and don't attempt to attend the show if you have a sneezing cat or if it has running eyes, or seems to be off colour. Do not show a female who is still nursing kittens, even if they are eight or ten weeks old because towards the end of the day her milk glands will swell to some extent, which will be uncomfortable for the cat and cause her to lose points. She may also be uneasy and object to being handled.

Previous page: left When you have to take your cat to see the vet a hold-all is useful to carry him in. Allow the cat's head to be free so he can see what is going on but care must be taken to fasten the top of the bag so he cannot wriggle out.

Right There is a mysterious lethal factor in the genetic pattern of Manx Cats. The true Manx, that is one with no tail whatsoever, is called a 'Rumpy'. There are Manx Cats of pure breeding with a little bit of a tail, these are called 'Stumpies'. When two Rumpies are mated the kittens often die at birth but when Stumpies are introduced into the breeding pattern this seems to eliminate the risk.

———

Left This mother cat is on a safari with her kittens. Perhaps for the young ones it is a first lesson in hunting. The cat's reactions and perceptions are amazingly swift and acute. The picture shows clearly that although the kittens are nervous, this can be seen by the way they carry their tails, they are tense and ready for action. For them the big adventure is only just beginning.

Don't be surprised if you are disappointed with your cat when you get to the show – all cats look well in their own homes, but often appear quite different in a show pen. The judge will always tell you, later in the day, just why it has failed, and one soon learns what is required in the various breeds. Let your cats and kittens be handled at home as much as possible; nervous cats who mistrust people are unhappy in shows. Most cats, however, love to show off and be told by the judges and visitors how beautiful they are.

Beginners tend to keep too many cats; they do not realize that cats and kittens must be constantly watched to keep them fit and happy. Once your female is in kitten, do not fuss her too much if she seems quite well; give her a good mixed diet, but do not overfeed her. The kittens should arrive from the 63rd to the 65th day, and the first litter is usually born on time, but as the cat gets older they sometimes go to 67, 68 and even 70 days before kittening. Keep in touch with a good vet is case anything goes wrong, and send for him if you are worried; only experience will give you confidence to deal with the kittens' arrival without help. Take advice from an experienced breeder, but keep as calm as possible or your cat may not settle. Some cats are very good mothers and give no trouble, others are not so efficient; one never knows how a cat will cope until the event happens. Give her a good bed away from the light; roomy fibre-glass indoor houses with a wire door can be bought for the purpose, and will be well worth the money. I also recommend a collapsible wire run for use when the kittens start to move about; they can be put in it for feeding and at night, or any time you may wish to have the kittens under control, such as your own meal times. Do not sell kittens under ten weeks of age; take as much care as possible to put them into good homes, and do not sell kittens abroad unless the would-be purchaser can be recommended.

If you cannot devote sufficient time to breeding, start with two neuters. They will be company for one another and if they are pedigree cats, can be registered and exhibited at shows in the neuter classes. If they are not pedigrees they can be exhibited at any show (such as the National Show, held at Olympia, London, every December), which has Household Pet classes. These always create great interest as there are Blacks, Whites, Tabbies of all colours, Blacks and Whites, Torties, Long-hairs and Short-hairs and they are judged by well-known people. One cat is usually chosen as the Best Household Pet, and if there are several classes there will be a Best Long-hair and Best Short-hair. Classes for kittens will be available also, and these are always a great centre of attraction.

Top left It is unkind to send a cat out at night, especially in bad weather. Staying in at night should be a matter of training, not compulsion. However, cats should be able to enjoy their freedom and be given access to the garden whenever they feel the need to do so. The simplest way to do this is to have a cat door fitted to one of the outside doors of the house.

Bottom left It is necessary for a cat to scratch in order to keep it's claws in perfect condition. As the outer shell of the claw becomes worn it needs to be pulled off, rather as we clip a broken finger nail. An ordinary log, complete with bark, is very suitable for this purpose but when prolonged use has worn it smooth it should be replaced with another.

Right A cat living in the country is likely to collect burrs in its coat. It can also pick up parasites from the grass, particularly if there are hedgehogs about. It is important to see that the cat enjoys a vigorous brushing every day to remove these nuisances from the coat. Before combing, run your hand over the cat's body to remove burrs. A fine comb will get through to the under fur to remove parasites. Give the first brushing against the lie of the coat, from tail to head, to remove loose hairs, then brush the hair down with long, sweeping strokes.

Left Your cat should be provided with her own dishes, brush and basket and these should be kept scrupulously clean. This is a family of Turkish Van cats, and they are obviously enjoying their basket. Once the kittens are more than three weeks old and are really beginning to grow it does not matter so much what sort of basket they have, but it is important to give the mother a well-ventilated, draught-free, warm basket or box when she is about to produce the kittens, in the hope that she will consent to use it. Without proper guidance she will invariably make for your best hat or the airing cupboard, which is never a good idea.

Below This adorable bundle bent on mischief is a litter of Siamese kittens. When born, these kittens are about the size of mice but they grow very quickly.

When the kittens are about a month old they begin to climb out of their box. It is very distracting to have these little charmers about and difficult to settle to serious matters. They like lots of attention, so talk to them quietly, for conversation is important. Kittens soon begin to understand the different tones of voice. Like babies they tire very quickly, so remember they require plenty of sleep.

Right Long-haired cats are considered by many to be the most beautiful of all but the long flowing coat does need a great deal of attention. Sometimes called Persians, these Long-haired Cats tend to have rather smaller litters of kittens, the size may vary from one to six but most often the number produced is three and this is a comfortable number for the queen to rear.

Top left It isn't true to say that cats can see in the dark but they can see better than most mammals in a dim light. The cat is a nocturnal animal so its eyes are adapted for hunting by moonlight. Many animals that are about when we are asleep can increase the amount of light passing into the retina because they have a reflecting layer behind. It is this reflecting layer that causes a cat's eyes to shine at night when a bright light is directed at them. One of the reasons the Ancient Egyptians regarded the cat as sacred was because they thought their eyes reflected the sun while it was hidden from Man.

Bottom left This cat lives at a brewery where horses are used to pull the drays. Warm, comfortable, and sweet smelling, the hay left for the horses supper makes an attractive bed and playground.

Above Siamese can sometimes look out of place when they are hunting outside in the grass, as their exotic colouring makes them very conspicuous – camouflage is out of the question. This is a Tabby Point Siamese, one of the more recent varieties to have appeared, and is very striking in colouring indeed.

Right It is believed that the cat's 'miaow' is reserved for their conversations with humans but when they talk to each other there are as many as a hundred different sounds and tones they can use. This kitten has obviously got something very urgent and secret to tell its mother.

The Orientals

When we think of the Oriental breeds, we mean the royal cats of Siam. With their inscrutable eyes of deep blue, their air of aloofness, their elegant bodies and their coats of sharply contrasting seal and fawn, they are unlike any other breed of cat. I write now of the original Seal Point variety, which is still a firm favourite in spite of the many other colour variations now seen in the Siamese breed.

Siamese cats came into England officially in 1884; a pair were a gift from the King of Siam to Mr Owen Gould, then the Consul General at Bangkok. He later gave them to his sister, Mrs Veley, who bred from them and later became a founder member of the Siamese Cat Club. Later two more were allowed to leave Siam for England, imported by Mrs Vyvyan and Miss Forester Walker. However, it is known that Siamese were exhibited at the Crystal Palace Show in 1871, and between that date and 1887 fifteen males and four females were shown. It would therefore appear that some had been smuggled into this country, in spite of the fact that the King of Siam was very concerned with true breeding and for many years allowed only a few cats to leave Bangkok with trusted people.

For several years breeders found these cats very delicate; they belonged exclusively to wealthy people, who mistakenly coddled them, keeping them in overheated rooms and not allowing a breath of air to blow over them. They were incorrectly fed and very prone to intestinal disorders, mainly due to worms from which they suffered acutely. Gradually, however, it was realized that Siamese were quite tough if they were allowed more freedom and fresh air, kept from draughts and damp, and fed sensibly. However, kittens always need special care and attention for the first six months of their life at least.

There are various legends about the Siamese cats. It is said that they were originally kept in the Royal palace as repositories for the souls of transmigrating Siamese Royalty. There is also a story about the kink in the tail (which incidentally is not liked at shows); a Princess of Siam hung her rings on her favourite cat's tail when she went bathing and the knot she tied so as not to loose them left the kink at the end. Whether there is any truth in these legends or not, they illustrate a long intimacy between these cats and humans, and nobody who has once been admitted into this intimacy can ever love any other animal quite so dearly.

Siamese cats are greedy, jealous and, I suppose, destructive, since any piece of fine embroidery exists in their minds only as a suitable toy for their claws. But these faults fade beside their charms: their sense of humour, their fidelity, their dauntless courage, their playfulness, their conversational powers, their honesty (by which I mean they will take your dinner off the table in front of you), their passionate interest in all that is going on around them and finally the depth of affection which they are able to show in so many exquisite ways. They are clever with their paws, opening catches on doors and windows quite easily with their strong claws, which, like the dog's, are never retracted.

I am sure that all those who love and know Siamese will agree with me and also appreciate their qualities to the full. Of all the breeds of cats Siamese must be kept happy and should never be confined in cages away from human contact as they love people and are intensely curious. If they are left alone for long periods they will become bored and get into mischief, looking for anything they can destroy and tear to bits, knocking things down, and often howling at the top of their voices. So if you do have to go out a lot it is always better to have two cats, or a cat and dog to keep each other company. They usually adopt one person in a household as their special friend, who may not be their actual owner. They get on well with other breeds of cats and with dogs if they are introduced to them as kittens. Unfortunately, some owners do not treat them well, especially those who hope to make money out of stud cats and brood queens. Too often they are crowded together and the females

are allowed to have too many kittens, which may result in anaemia and early death.

For many years Blue and Chocolate Points were comparatively rare. Gradually the Blues increased and were recognized by the GCCF as a separate colour in 1936. The Chocolate Points gained recognition in 1951, and in 1961 the Lilac Points (called Frost Points in America) became the fourth colour variation. There are now Red Points, Tabby Points and Tortie Points as well, and these have been evolved by mating to the British Cats. The standard has changed over the years; in the early days the face of the Siamese was much rounder than it is now, and some breeders are beginning to think that the breeding of cats with a very pointed face has gone too far and that the cats are loosing their good chin shape. However, the American Standard for Siamese favours even narrower heads and longer, thinner bodies. Siamese are meant to be fairly heavy cats, especially the males; females should not be too small, or it will be difficult for them to produce healthy kittens, and thin, scrawny kittens will be nervy and have little power of resistance when ill.

Siamese cats are very demanding, and although they should live as unrestricted a life as possible, care should be taken to treat them sensibly. Do not spoil them or they may rule you and your household. Never neglect any signs of illness as Siamese are the most difficult invalids; they cannot bear to be ill and sometimes lack the will to live. If your pet is ill, never leave it to the care of other people, as knowing you are there will do much to ensure their recovery.

Previous page: left Lilac-Point Siamese are known in the United States of America as Frost-Points. The mask and points are a pinkish grey, the ears are almost transparent but when the light shows through them they are a lovely shade of lavender. The coat should be of a pale magnolia shade.

Right One of the very latest Siamese cats to receive recognition by The Governing Council of the Cat Fancy is the Tabby Point. From time to time tabby markings appear in all breeds of cats because the gene for tabby is dominant. Careful breeding has now made it possible to control the tabby marking and this attractive cat is the result.

Top left The regal demeanour of this Siamese reminds us that in Ancient Egypt the cat was revered and worshipped. It is probably from the name of the Cat Goddess 'Bast' or 'Pasht' that we get the diminutive 'Puss'. The Egyptians built a shrine to honour the cat-headed goddess on an island completely surrounded by water. This was probably to keep her from straying.

Bottom left A story is told of the Princess of Siam who long ago went to bathe in the river. Not knowing where to leave her valuable rings, she hooked them over the tail of her pet cat. All was well until the cat chased a butterfly and the rings fell off. The next time she went to bathe she tied a knot in the cat's tail so she would not lose the rings. When she returned the rings were safely in place but even today some Siamese have a kink in the tail as a result of the knot.

Right The Abyssinian cat is said to resemble the cats worshipped by the Egyptians long ago and also the Caffre cat from which the early domestic cats were descended. Their coat pattern is unusual in that each hair has two or three separate bands of colour on it; the ground colour is a russet brown, the bands are black or dark brown. However, there should be no banding on the inside of the forelegs and belly. This kitten is a very good specimen, as he has the correct cream coloured chin, and virtually no tabby markings which many Abyssinians have on their legs and tails.

Left Siamese kittens are pure white when they are born. When they are about a week old the points will begin to darken and by the time they are a month old they will be recognizable as Siamese. These kittens have quite definitely established themselves as Seal Point and Chocolate Point Siamese.

Below This proud Chocolate Point Siamese with her small family is a very new mother. By their tiny white faces it can be seen that the kittens are very young. Like all kittens they are born blind but Siamese kittens begin to open their eyes when they are about three days old.

Right This Siamese Seal Point really has her hands full with this litter of kittens. The breed averages five kittens in a litter, although some have been known to have seven or eight. Five is really all she can manage, particularly when they grow large.

Below The Cat Fanciers Association in America does not yet recognize the Blue Burmese, although it is recognized in Britain. The body should be predominantly bluish grey, darker on back, with a silver sheen to the coat. Ears, mask and points shade to silver grey.

Right The Burmese is the only natural breed of brown cats, the originals were the result of natural mating. When one was taken to the United States it was considered attractive enough for someone to begin breeding it and so it was mated with a Siamese. The Burmese should be a really dark shade of seal.

Above is a group of Red Point Siamese all wondering what the photographer is doing. This is a new breed to be accepted in Britian. When they conform to the standard they are very striking but there is difficulty still in eliminating the rings from their tails. These kittens are only nine weeks old but already the tails bear the marks of their Red Tabby heritage.

Left Seal Point Siamese were the earliest variety whilst Blue Points were comparatively rare. The Seal Point in this picture shows clearly the requirements in a good specimen. The well-proportioned head, narrowing to a fine muzzle with width between the eyes, the mask, ears, feet and tail dense and clearly defined, the oval paws and extra long tail all gain points for the show cat. Siamese often have a tendency to squint, then the eyes are placed so that they appear to look permanently at the nose. This is considered a fault and would lose points.

Right There are fewer Siamese cats in Siam than there are in many European countries. The Siamese people often refer to it as the 'Chinese cat'. The first importations to appear in this country were the Seal Point, with the dark brown markings, which this young specimen displays on his mask, ears and paws.

Big Cats

Most of the Big Cats live in Asia and are classed with the Domestic Cats in a group called Felidae. The best known are the Lion, Leopard, Tiger, Puma, Cheetah, Jaguar and Ocelot; specimens of these breeds can be seen in the big zoos at home and abroad and in the wild life reservations which various governments have set up to preserve them. An exception is the Snow Leopard, which is found in Tibet. The Puma is native to both North and South America, and is also called the Mountain Lion. The Cheetah, said to be the fastest animal in the world, can be domesticated but has never been known to breed in captivity.

The Lynx is a smaller wild cat and is found in many places. The African Lynx has large ears with tufts of hair at the tips; the coat colour is pale, rusty red to grey. It is said that the Abyssinian cat is descended from the African Lynx and the tufted ears, the coat colour, and the ability to swim support this theory. On the other hand, the Abyssinian cat is often called the Little Lion because of its resemblance to the lioness in colour, expression, and coat pattern. The Tabby cat has been likened to the Tiger and the Leopard to the Indian desert cat, which has a spotted yellow coat and is probably one of the ancestors of our Spotted domestic cat. Another close relative to domestic cats could be the African Kaffir cat, which is yellow in colour and known to mate with domestics. It is interesting to note that the Big Cats are short-haired, like the Wild and domestic cat. The exceptions are the Lion, with his mane of long hair, and the Pallas Cat, which has a long coat and bushy tail.

We cannot be certain when cats came to Britain, but people who have carefully studied the subject are sure that they were brought by the Romans, who regarded them as prized possessions. However it is probable the European wild cat, Felis Sylvestris, was already established. Today the Scottish Wild Cat, Felis Sylvestris Grampia, is on the increase in Scotland. They are quite untamable, even kittens found abandoned are spitting bundles of fury and cannot be tamed even from such an early age. A few wild cats are known to have mated with domestic cats, probably the wilder type found on isolated farms. The Scottish Wild Cats are larger than domestic ones; they have larger, flatter heads and their ears often turn downwards, probably a natural protection.

During the last ten years domestic cats with folded ears have appeared on a farm in Scotland; these are a mutation and may be the result of matings between a wild cat and a feral farm cat. The litters are usually mixed, some having ordinary ears. It is claimed that the folded-ear cats are sometimes deaf and the majority of breeders consider them abnormal. A few interested people would like them recognized as a new breed, but it is unlikely that the Governing Council of the Cat Fancy will agree to do so.

During the last war many cats fled from bombed areas and became wild, living on bomb sites and in wooded areas, fending for themselves. Many were rescued and became tame again, some had to be trapped and destroyed, and many others died from exposure and neglect. There are stories of these poor cats who crawled into people's outhouses to die, having the instinct to get among humans again.

Cats have had a chequered existence, loved by some, hated by others. Fussed over, revered and pampered in ancient times, they were later treated with the utmost cruelty in the Middle Ages because they were coupled with witches and black magic. Today many have loving owners and good homes, but many more are thrown out to roam the streets, all too often meeting a fate worse than death in a laboratory. Cats are beautiful and clever animals; but they are independent and do not appeal to the people who prefer the utter devotion of a dog, which will make noisy demands upon its owner. Cats have a sense of direction and can find their way back to their homes and owners, covering many miles; although they may appear aloof they can be very devoted.

Previous page: left Cats love warmth and the greater variety of cats live in warmer climates. One of the few exceptions is the Snow Leopard. This Big Cat is found on the snowy heights of Tibet where it is protected by an ample furry coat. Unfortunately the lovely coat has been coveted by fashion conscious ladies and the numbers of Snow Leopards has become dangerously depleted.

Right The Lion differs in appearance from other cats. The male Lion has long hair on his head and shoulders, this is his mane. He also has a tuft of hair on the end of his tail. Female Lions do not have these adornments, they look more like other cats. Lions are, of course, the largest, heaviest, and most powerful of all the cat family, but they can be quite easily frightened.

Below left The Lion and the Tiger are both the largest and heaviest of all the cats. Their weight is too great for them to be expert climbers. The Cheetah is the fastest of all mammals and relies on speed rather than the refuge of a tree. All other cats are expert climbers. It is part of their natural caution that they often find a favourite place on top of a garden shed or in the branches of a tree where they can be safe from intrusion and can watch for anything stirring below. This little kitten is very curious to see who is invading his sanctuary in the branches.

Below right Except for Lions the Big Cats are rarely seen. Unless they are in a tight spot, or are defending their young, they seldom attack men. Most Big Cats live alone or hunt in pairs. This Jungle Cat has found a place where his camouflage is almost perfect, and with the sun dappling his coat he would be very difficult to see.

Right The Leopards spots are mainly arranged in rosettes. It is surprising how many and varied are the spot patterns in cats. There are large spots and small spots, some are round, some oblong. The Jaguar has spots within spots, in his rosette there is one spot and sometimes more. A Cheetah has single spots like a bad attack of measles.

Left Although the cats who live in a colony in the Forum live really as wild cats their well-being lacks nothing, as you can see by the appearance of this cat lying in the shade of a tomb. He is well fed and relaxed. Cats were introduced to Rome, it is supposed, by the Egyptians. It is also reasonable to suppose that the cat was brought to Britain by the Romans. The evidence to support this lies in the fact that clear imprints of cats' paws have been found in tiles in Roman villas built during the first centuries of the Christian era.

Below A Cheetah and her two cubs. These, the fastest of all the mammals, have more dog-like characteristics than any of the other cats, and also have very distinctive markings, with striking 'tear stripes' running down their faces from the corner of the eyes to the end of the nose.

Bottom right Lion cubs are born fully furred and have grey spots and rosettes, which fade as they grow older. Their eyes probably open fully when they are about two weeks old, and at six months old they begin to join their mother out hunting. A lioness has to teach her cubs how to stalk and kill their prey, how to follow the pride and generally fend for themselves. The young lioness **right** will have nearly reached her full strength, and one blow from her paw will kill a zebra or an antelope.

Right The Wild Cat was common in Britain until the early nineteenth century. When firearms were introduced and forests were cleared the Wild Cat was brought almost to extinction, except in Scotland where it is on the increase. Although Felis Sylvestris resembles the domesticated tabby, the Wild Cat is more heavily built. The head of the Wild Cat is broad and square with abundant whiskers, the fur is thicker than that of the domestic tabby and the tail ends with a blunt tip, unlike that of the domestic cat which tapers to a point.

It lives in the thickly wooded areas in the Highlands where it can find protection among the rocks and trees. Since it has increased in numbers it has begun to move further south.

The teeth of all cats, wild or domesticated, are developed to give a firm hold on struggling prey. They are sharpened into scissor like blades which can pare meat from a bone.

Cat lived on earth many millions of years before Man. It is possible to confirm this fact from the skeletal remains of the extinct Sabre-toothed Tiger of prehistoric times. A skull of one of these animals was found in a cave in Brazil, it is similar to the cat of today in its teeth formation. There are six teeth at the top front, these are very small and simple, six teeth grow in the lower jaw but they are even smaller. The next tooth on either side in each jaw is the large, strong conical tooth, these teeth are curved and sharply pointed. The small size of the front teeth in contrast, makes the larger teeth look quite fearsome.

Left Looking at this Tiger lying peacefully in the sun it is hard to imagine the pent up fury that you would unleash if you dared to invade his privacy. The Tiger can be as gentle as a kitten, purring and playing in exactly the same way as your fireside pet.

Below There is a saying which goes 'One needs to watch the cat at work to see the tiger in the hearth.' When you are sitting with puss curled up on your knee it is difficult to imagine that he can be alert to every movement. When the moment is right, quick as a flash every muscle will spring into action and a lightning paw will shoot out with deadly aim on some unsuspecting prey.

Right One of the small wild cats of America, the Ocelot is becoming increasingly popular as a pet. They are easily tamed and make intelligent, playful and absorbing companions. As can be seen, they are extremely decorative, even if rather more alarming at first sight than the domestic cat.

Showing

The best way to become known in the English Cat Fancy is by exhibiting your cats at the shows. In Britain they are held under the jurisdiction of the Governing Council of the Cat Fancy, which issues licences to clubs to hold shows, providing they are affiliated to the Governing Council and are prepared to obey rules laid down by this body. There are three types of show – Exemption, Sanction and Championship. Exemption shows are very good to attend and exhibit at if you are a beginner, as although the general rules are greatly relaxed, professional judges will be officiating and you can get from them a valuable assessment of your cat, kitten or neuter, and of your non-pedigree cats as well. You can compare your exhibits with others, join the Club and get to know other owners who will soon help you with plenty of advice. Sanction shows are rehearsals for shows with Championship status, so everything must be carried out as at a Championship show. At a Championship show official judges are empowered to award or withhold championship certificates, and your cat will need three, awarded by different judges of the breed at three different shows in order to become a champion.

If you mean to show your cat it is essential that he should be used to being handled and not prone to becoming nervous or aggressive when put into a pen. Most cats love shows and thoroughly enjoy being told how beautiful they are. But occasionally you get a cat who appears to suffer from claustrophobia, refuses point blank to be removed from his pen and flies at the unlucky judge or steward who attempts to handle him. If your cat is like this, accept it. Do not show him again or he will get a reputation for bad temper that he probably does not deserve. It is against the rules to give a cat sedatives, so accept the situation to save yourself and others real trouble. Some people think that a stud cat will not be used if he does not become a champion, or that kittens will not be bought if the queen is not a champion. This is a fallacy, for it is known that cats attaining this status are not always the best breeders, likewise many unshown cats breed winning kittens, provided they are well bred themselves.

A pedigree cat is one whose ancestors are known for at least three or four generations. To enter a show licensed by the GCCF a cat or kitten must be registered, and once a cat is registered it must not be entered in an unlicensed show without permission from the Council. Household cats need not be registered and can be entered in the special classes provided for them. Registered neuters can also compete for Premier certificates at Championship Shows, but only cats can compete for challenge certificates. Single kittens may not be exhibited until they are at least three months old, except at a few summer shows, where they may be accepted at eight weeks. Single Siamese and Burmese kittens, however, are not accepted under the age of four months. Many shows have litter classes for three or more kittens from the same litter between the ages of ten and twelve weeks, though some shows have discontinued these classes. A kitten becomes a cat at nine months.

Never attempt to show a cat that is out of condition or not well groomed. Long-hairs need a great deal of preparation. Brush and comb your cat or kitten every day so that only the finishing touches are needed on show day. Long-haired Blacks, Reds and Brown Tabbies need to be cleaned with cotton wool pads soaked in eau-de-cologne. Points are lost for a Long-haired or Short-haired White if it has a stained yellow tail. These cats need to be powdered carefully, and sometimes bathed before a show. Before undertaking this, get some advice from people who deal with these particular breeds. Powder must not be left in a cat's coat for judging, and it is against the rules to brush it out in the hall on the morning of the show. Short-haired cats need grooming also, and Siamese benefit from an overnight bran bath. Daily hand grooming cannot be bettered for all Short-haired breeds, as their coats lie flat, whereas the Long-

hairs' coats are brushed upwards towards the head and should never be smoothed down flat. The most popular breeds of cats are the Long-haired Blues, Siamese and Burmese, and it is in their classes that the most competition will be found. If you are disappointed to find your cat has not won an award, especially if you feel he is just as good as the cats which did, you can ask the judge if she will tell you from her notes her opinion of your cat. This will be helpful, and show you just where your cat failed.

Continental cat shows have been held in various parts of the Continent and Scandinavia since 1924, and since 1950 the number of shows has greatly increased.

Their method differs from the British and the American style in many ways. Cat shows in Australia and New Zealand are run on the same principle as those in Britain, but one-day shows are more popular. The American Cat Fancy is much larger than the British and there are several Governing Bodies in the various States and many clubs catering for all breeds. Show procedure is very different from the English and Continental methods; the judging method is unique and it is difficult to qualify as a judge.

A feature of the Continental and Scandinavian shows is the two or three day 'exposition'. The last day is usually a Sunday, and in most places the gate is enor-

mous, with crowds milling around the hall all day. Members only exhibit; they have their own pens, transporting them to and from the show; no entry fees are paid and there is no prize money. All exhibits receive a certificate signed by the judge and at the end of the last day prizes are presented, some very beautiful and valuable. These are donated by Patrons, Officers, Committee members and friends. Every exhibitor gets a prize and some lucky winners receive several gifts. Pens are decorated before the show opens; coloured curtains and cushions and flower arrangements make a colourful and interesting display which the public appreciate and enjoy.

Previous page: left The Russian Blue was once called the Archangel Blue. Some say they used to be the pets of the Tsars of Russia but others deny there is a trace of Russian blood in them. The Russian Blue is longer in the leg than the British cat, and finer boned.

Right The Brown Tabby in the picture looks rather sad. Perhaps it is because it is a breed that has lost its popularity and as a result there are very few breeders. One of the faults, and a persistent one, is the white chin. It is taking breeders a long time to eradicate it from the Brown Tabby.

Left Colourpoints are now being bred in all the various Siamese colourings, and this is a Red Colourpoint kitten, posing elegantly for his photograph among the nasturtiums. To many people these are the ideal cats, as they combine the popular Siamese colouring with the Persian type. In America they are known as Himalayan cats, and the Red Point is recognized by the American Cat Fancy, though not by the British organization.

Below The Red Tabby is one of the most attractive Short-hairs and for show purposes the background colour should be a really rich red, while the markings must be a distinctly darker shade. This kitten is well marked and the coat will darken as it grows older.

Right Portrait of a Tabby Point Siamese. These beautiful cats are real 'show stoppers' as they have pale bodies with tabby points, fine, well ringed tails with solid black tips, black stockings up the backs of the hind legs and wide ears with black 'thumb marks' at the back. This cat is in first class condition and his bright eyes and alert appearance give every indication of his energy and good health.

Below It took years of breeding to produce a Chestnut-Brown. This cat was once known in Britain as the Havana. The name was dropped to prevent wild stories from circulating about its origin. In the United States of America the cat is still known as Havana. It is a rich, warm brown, mahogany hue all over. It is a foreign type cat with slanting oriental eyes.

Bottom Taillessness, height of hindquarters, shortness of back and depth of flank are essentials in a Manx Cat. It is a combination of these features which give this cat its rabbity gait. The double coat is also like that of a rabbit. The undercoat is very thick and soft and there is another thick coat of long hairs as well. The Manx characteristics are important to show judges because colour and marking are a secondary consideration.

Right This beautiful Chinchilla in all her elegant splendour is a fine example of her breed. In the early years of her ancestry the eye colour was immaterial and a brown eye of any shade, which was once permissible, is now a disqualification in a show. The emerald, or blue-green, which is now required by the standard, is very attractive and is enhanced by the contrast with the silvery sparkle of the coat.

Above The Smoke Cat, as a breed, is almost disappearing. It is being replaced by the Blues, Creams and Chinchillas. The Smoke is recognized in two colours, Blue and Black, and should be a cat of contrasts. The undercoat should be as light as possible with the tips shading to black. The dark parts should be emphasised on the back, head and feet.

Left Until the last century all cats in the Western Hemisphere had short thick coats. Cats with long hair existed in Persia several centuries before this. Breeders interested in introducing a longer coated cat imported some of these cats from Persia. First they were taken to France, then later they came to England to improve the length of hair in the English cats. At first this new breed was known as Angora but at a later date it was changed to Persian. Now they are just called 'Long-hairs'. This little kitten has yet to grow his magnificent coat and the flowing ruff which is typical of these cats.

Right The Cream Short-hair is rare at shows. Perhaps because its colour must be a rich cream, there must be no sign of white and it must be free from bars. Quite often kittens are like this when they are really young, only to develop bars on the legs and rings on the tail as they grow.

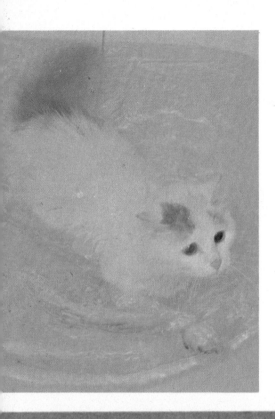

Left The Turkish Van cats are the only breed that seem to really enjoy swimming – usually cats hate water.

Right It is very difficult to achieve even patching in a Tortoiseshell and White cat and this is not a perfect show specimen but it is in its favour that the patches are clearly defined.

Below This Rex cat is showing his fine marcel-like waves. Each individual hair is waved. The guard hairs are shortened to just below the level of the top coat so there are none visible. Even the whiskers and eyebrows are crinkled. The Cornish cat has a thicker coat than the Devon.

Below centre The Red Abyssinian is known in The United States as 'Sorrel'. The colour should be rich copper red, ticked with bands of darker colour. Many people believe the Abyssinian may be descended from the Egyptian sacred cats, as the type is very similar to

those seen in illustrations in museums.

Left Cats love to find a sunny spot by a brick wall where the warm stonework will act as a suntrap. Any moment now this cat will curl up and go to sleep.

Right The British Blue has been described by some people as the aristocrat of British Short-hairs. The blueness of the coat is most attractive when it is of a medium shade and it is important that the coat should be really short.

Below The Blue-Cream Long-hair is a difficult cat to breed because the colours must be softly intermingled and the overall effect should present the appearance of shot silk. Another obstacle is the fact that, like Tortoiseshells, Blue-Cream males are rare. Breeding from this variety is something of a lottery as the kittens are unpredictable. It is not surprising, under the circumstances, to find a scarcity at the shows.

Cats Alone

Almost everyone who has a pet will need to make use of a boarding kennels at holiday time or in cases of special emergency. If you are interested and concerned about your cat you will want to look at all the available accommodation in your district and, even if you are recommended to a place, do not arrange to take your pet there until you have first inspected it. When you find a place you like, and that your cat subsequently also likes stick to it so that your cat will become familiar with the surroundings and the people in charge.

If you have a cat that is very settled in its habits you may have a friend who will go in twice a day to feed the cat and change its tray. Never leave it to fend for itself and never leave a cat behind unprotected if you move house or leave the district. If you cannot take the cat and are unable to find it a suitable home it is better to have it painlessly put to sleep. (See the cat after this has been done to avoid any mistake.) If you can find the cat a home, please make sure it is suitable. People often say they will take a cat, but if it does not settle down quickly or seem to be fond of them, they may become impatient with it and neglect it. Some cats are un-

doubtedly unhappy at leaving their familiar home and may miss a particular person very much. A cat may be scared of another cat, dog or child in the new place, be afraid to move about much and so may become dirty. Many people have told me that they will not have it on their conscience that they had a healthy animal put to sleep, but they do not stop to consider that by giving it away they may be condemning it to a worse fate.

No-one should start a boarding establishment for animals unless they have some knowledge of them. Cats are often quite happy the first week they are away, for the change of scene and people will interest them. If they are going to become mopey it usually shows itself in the second week. This is the time that they are most likely to pick up any infection, so the place where you leave your cat should have runs divided from one another by a solid partition as well as wire netting. This prevents direct contact with a sneezing cat, if there should be one there. In the best type of boarding kennels the houses will not be under one roof. The house should have a sleeping compartment, a shelf under a window and a door for the cat to get in and out at

will. Heating should be available for cold nights and for winter boarding if required.

A deep sanitary tray should be provided. If possible, runs should be of concrete with a pot of grass for the cat. Make sure fastenings on doors and windows are safe, for many a cat has escaped from a run-down place. Let your cat have its own blanket and favourite toy. If there is room for the cat's box or basket, it may settle down more readily if it can sleep in it. On the whole cats and kittens are happy in catteries and eat well, and they soon know if they are well looked after. Do not attempt to take your cat if it is not well, as it is not fair on the owners nor on the other cats. Most kennel owners require a veterinary certificate to say that your pet has been inoculated against feline enteritis. Give the owner a diet sheet and be sure and tell the cattery owner if your cat has any awkward ways, such as biting ankles, or is difficult over grooming, and so on. Be sure your cat has clean ears and coat free from fleas or other pests. Leave your address and be sure to say 'Goodbye' to your pet and assure him that you will soon be back, as cats are hypersensitive and really do understand what is going on around them.

However much you love your cat I would not advise you to go without a holiday because you think your cat's way of life must not be disturbed. Some people put animals into the same category as humans, but this is wrong. They cannot think as we do, but if it really makes you unhappy to go away without your pet, arrange a holiday in a caravan or country cottage. Some boarding houses and hotels will take cats, but not very many.

People who run good kennels do make an income, but the work is hard and never finished. One has to be on hand all the time,

and it is too much work for one person, as you will find that to board only half a dozen cats will take up a great deal of time. Cleaning houses, cooking and preparing food, washing dishes and blankets, putting down fresh water and changing sanitary trays at least twice a day all makes a lot of work. So do not undertake this way of making money unless you are dedicated to cats' welfare.

Cruelty to animals is a terrible thing. It is possible that cruelty to cats is more evident than to any other animal, although all suffer in their various ways. There are now numerous welfare societies for the protection of cats, though cats nowadays are often treated as badly as they were a hundred years ago. People still have to be urged not to desert cats when they move house or go on holiday, not to let children torment them, and not to ill-treat or starve them. Cats nowadays face even greater hazards from the cat stealers. These wicked people pick up healthy cats who may be crossing the road, or sunning themselves in their own gardens, and sell them to dealers who turn them over to laboratories for experimental purposes. Goodness knows what the fate is of many of them. Dogs are protected by law in a way that does not apply to cats; a stray dog or one that is run over in the road must be taken to a police station for a report to be made, but not so a cat. It is all the more important, therefore, for us to take extra care of our pets.

Previous page: left Silver Tabbies are one of the most popular breeds of all, as their markings are particularly striking. A correctly marked Tabby is hard to breed, as very precise rules have been established as to the ringing and marking. Any Tabby is a beautiful cat, but the Silver is outstanding because of the light and sparkling background colour of the coat.

Right Cats are capable of great devotion both to each other and to their owners, and if two from the same litter have the good fortune to live their lives together they will probably be inseparable. Kittens form attachments at a very early age, and too often pairs are split up and sent to different homes. These two Tortoiseshell cats may quarrel and fight occasionally, but on the whole there is nothing they will not do for each other.

Top left In busy Baghdad where the Arabs crowded the famous silk bazaar, cats were to be seen all around. The name of the bazaar was Attabiah, after the watered silk which was made there. Since the pattern of the cats resembled the effect of the silk the name 'tabby' was attached to these brindled cats.

Top right It isn't really quite the thing to do, to hide in the skin of your distant relative. This little kitten only knows that it is soft and comfortable, and that this tiger skin definitely matches his colouring.

Left Although there are so many beautiful varieties from which to choose, most household pets conform to no particular standards for cats. They are the mongrel offspring of centuries of free mating, cats are notoriously promiscuous. This does not make them less charming and lovable, as cats possess a beauty all their own.

Right Cats are natural predators and hunt for sport. It is a mistaken idea to suppose that a cat will make a better mouser if it is kept hungry. A cat or kitten that is fed regularly will have more vitality and stamina to do the job. Often the cat will earn the dislike of bird lovers when it kills small birds but the percentage of birds killed and eaten is lower than that of rodents and insects. Cats are classed as wild animals and the owner of a cat cannot be held responsible for the misdeeds of his pet.

Left and below Cats adore flattery and love being told they are beautiful. Most cat photographs look as if they are posed but it is in fact difficult to make a cat do something because you want it to, and poise is in its nature. Somehow the cat has a knack for finding surroundings complimentary to its own beauty. It can often be found in the garden among the brightest flowers and it seems to choose the colours which go best with its own coat colour. The colour of this orange and white bi-coloured cat is cleverly accentuated by the gold of the crocuses, and the little white and tabby kitten is seen to advantage against the cool colours of the mauve crocuses. It is this instinctive feeling for composition that makes the cat such a suitable subject for calendar pictures, chocolate box tops and birthday cards.

Right Cats have an aura and mystique all their own – it is often very hard to tell what a cat is thinking, and the aloof yet endearing look on this Tabby's face is baffling. He appears to be relaxed and pensive as he sunbathes on a bench, yet at any moment he could give you an intimidating stare, or a swipe with a powerful paw. The independence and inscrutability of cats is one of their main attractions.

Acknowledgements

The publishers would like to thank the following individuals and organizations for their kind permission to reproduce the pictures in this book:

Barnaby's Picture Library 8 top, 12 bottom, 46, 47, 49 bottom, 54 top, 58 bottom, 65 top right; Bruce Coleman 45, 59; *Camera Press* 14, 25, 28/29, 30 bottom, 51 bottom, 71; *Creszentia and Ted Allen* 16 top, 17, 18 top and bottom, 21 bottom, 44 bottom, 56, 57, 60 bottom, 61, 64 bottom; *Fox Photos* 68 top right; Friese, Paul *Z E F A* 54 bottom; Frohlich, K-D *Z E F A* 64 top right; Grossauer, J *Z E F A* 7, 12 top; Green, Will 33 top, 60 top left, 65 top left, 67, 70 bottom; Halliday, Sonia 32, 64 top left; Helmlinger, H *Z E F A* 69; Kalt, Gerolf *Z E F A* 34 top; Lewis, Gary C *Z E F A* 31; Litwin, Wallis *Photo Trends* 50 top; *Natural Science Photos* 50 bottom, 52/53, 55; *Octopus Books* 23, 38; Park, F *Z E F A* 21 top, 33 bottom; *Pictorial Press* 20, 58 top, 63; Sally Anne Thompson 4, 5, 10, 11, 15, 19, 22, 24 bottom, 27, 35, 36, 37, 39, 40, 42, 43, 44 top, 62 top, 65 bottom, 66, 67 left, 68 top left and bottom; *Spectrum* 6, 8 bottom, 9, 13, 24 top, 26, 30 top, 34 bottom, 49 top, 51 top, 70 top; *Syndication International* 16 bottom, 48; Thorlichen, G *Z E F A* 62 bottom; Wiesner, Hed *Z E F A* 41, 64/65.

First English edition published 1972 by
Octopus Books Limited
59 Grosvenor Street
London W1

© M C M L X X II Octopus Books Limited

Library of Congress Catalog Card Number 79-84559

All rights reserved
This edition is published by Crescent Books
A division of Crown Publishers Inc.

A B C D E F G H
Produced by Mandarin Publishers Limited
22A Westlands Road, Quarry Bay, Hong Kong

Printed in Hong Kong